YOU SAID WHAT?

EFFECTIVE COMMUNICATION SKILLS

HOW TO GET WHAT
YOU WANT THROUGH
EFFECTIVE COMMUNICATION

WAYNE SUTTON, LCCC

www.CoachingWithWayne.com

You Said What?

Effective Communication Skills
How to get what you want through effective communication

Wayne Sutton, LCCC
www.CoachingWithWayne.com

Table of Contents

Introduction

A partner of a leading firm comes back to his office and says to his manager, *"Did you get my message where I said, 'Ship the Enron documents to the Feds?'"* The manager goes white. *"Oh My God! I thought you said rip the Enron documents to shreds!"*

That's what happens when there is an error in communication. How can you make sure it never happens?

Communication is without doubt the most important skill required to live successfully. The world around you is competitive to say the least. Whether at home or at the workplace, at a mall, or with friends, if you can communicate well, you have got most things going your way. People do not just listen to a good communicator; they are ready to bend or unbend to the person's needs.

Not everybody is privileged to gain communication skills from the word 'go'. However, all one needs is a goal to become a successful communicator and find the right source to pick up the skills, half the job is done.

One such source from where you can pick up communication skills from scratch or refine those you already have is this "Effective Communication Skills" e-course.

This e-course is divided into 6 modules inclusive of exercises and assignments that will teach you the essence of effective communication and enable you to express yourself more clearly and confidently. Moreover, the modules are simple and going through this course will be smooth-sailing.

Now go ahead, and COMMUNICATE!

Understanding The Communications Process – How Does Miscommunication Occur?

Communication is vital to all of us, for without this skill we will be quite helpless and the world around us would be blank. After all every person, be it a worker, manager or a teenager, have interactions with other people almost all throughout their life.

It is easy to tell a person to do a task but the person may not interpret your command properly, thus resulting in a task that may not match your exact requirements.

That is where the difference between communicating and communicating effectively becomes apparent.

Always remember that an <u>effective communication goes far beyond the words you say</u>. For a communication process to be effective, one has to know the other person's views and the style of absorbing information.

In short, if you want to convey your message across to the other persons' mind, you need to adopt a style and approach that will evoke the desired response.

Effective communicators are well versed in the action signals and communication strategies that can be brought out from a person and adopt their style to make sure that their communications are effective.

In this chapter we will cover the basic process of communication and the issues that lead to miscommunication.

Before we go ahead, how about we do an exercise? After all it is practice that makes one perfect.

*EXERCISE

Take a blank piece of paper and write your name in the middle and then around your name write down the names of people with whom you have frequent communication or communication. This list will include friends, family, work colleagues, etc.

As you work through this course keep referring back to this diagram of the people whom you interact with the most and apply what you learn from them as individuals. Effective communication is all about tailoring your communication strategy for different people. NO TWO PEOPLE ARE ALIKE!

The Communication Process

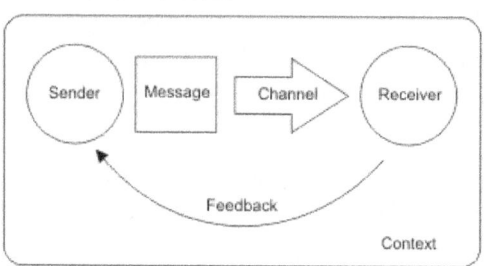

The Communications Process

The purpose of communication is to get your message across to others. This is a process that involves exchanging information between a sender and a receiver. Communication is the process of exchanging information through a common system of symbols, signs, behavior, speech, writing and signals.

Let us analyze how this exchange works.

To start the exchange we need a sender who has information that needs to be conveyed and then we need a receiver who is to accept this information.

Now the sender prepares the information in an organized manner and passes it to the receiver through a proper channel (text, speech etc).

So that's how easy it is! Just think, arrange and express!

Easy it is but the process leaves room for error, often causing unnecessary confusion and counter productivity between the sender and the receiver.

Say, for instance the case of an employee you heard "You are fired!!" instead of "You are hired!!"

Let's consider the incident we mentioned at the beginning of this course- the business partner and his manager. The conversation was a very simple one but because of certain discrepancies ending up with disastrous consequences. So where did it all go haywire?

In that particular episode, the partner (sender) wanted the documents shipped to the feds (information). Now according to the definition the sender has arranged his information in an organized manner and passed it onto the receiver (the manager). Now the receiver seems to have got the message but he had a rather distorted interpretation of the message.

Let us bring up the partner and his thought process that lead to this conversation.

He thinks of the idea "ship the documents to Feds" then he represents this thought in form words or text and expresses it through speech.

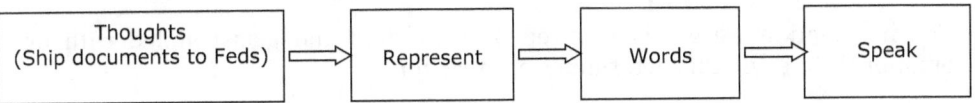

Well so far so good.

Enter the manager into this conversation and unfortunately the communication leads to a disaster!

The manager receives the message and he interprets ship as rip and fed as shred! And comprehends the message as "Rip the documents to shreds".

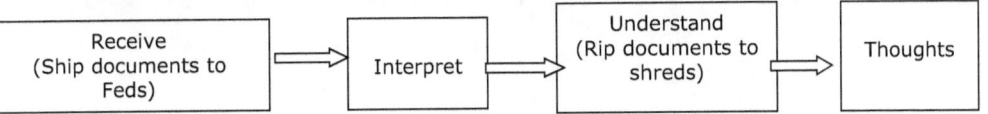

Here the information underwent a total change during the receiver's interpretation.

This misunderstanding of information could have happened due to the internal filter system of the person or the environment in which the information exchanges took place.

Now what is an internal filter? The name may sound new but internal filters are a vital system for every one of us.

The internal filter within each person decides the way we look at the world. These filters are basically sensory input channels like visual system, auditory system and kinesthetic system.

Here's an idea of what these input channels do:

Visual system helps us study and analyze the body language and physiology of others.

Auditory system enables us to hear the words spoken and the tones in which others speak.

Kinesthetic system is split into internal and external feelings. Internal feelings include feelings like hunger, stress, tension, comfort, pleasure etc. External feelings include touching someone or something, what it feels like – texture, pressure etc.

Based on our experiences, the filters create internal, mental maps of reality. When we communicate, whether through gestures and actions or verbally through language, we do so, based on our mental maps.

The information we get is received by the filters and gets coupled with our emotional state and this determines our reactions.

Now let us see how the filters influence our understanding of a message and our reactions.

Understanding information and reactions

Now let us look at another example:

Cary Grant is said to have been reluctant to reveal his age to the public, having played the youthful lover for more years than would have been appropriate. One day, while he was sorting out some business with his agent, a telegram arrived from a journalist who was desperate to learn how old the actor was. It read:

HOW OLD CARY GRANT?

Grant, who happened to open it himself, immediately cabled back:

OLD CARY GRANT FINE. HOW YOU?

What do you analyze from this example?

It looks like Cary Grant got the message clearly but he deduced the question's purpose and answered it in a totally different manner.

Now how did that happen?

When we get information, it is analyzed and modified in our mind in relation to the ideas and thoughts that linger in our mind. So when a person receives a message, he/she interprets the message in their preferred wording and language.

Our understanding is mainly influenced by a certain filters, to be precise, 6 filters.

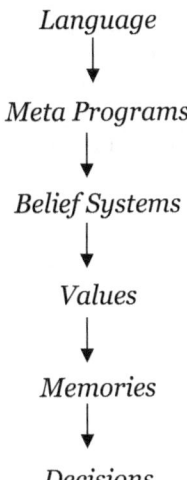

Language

↓

Meta Programs

↓

Belief Systems

↓

Values

↓

Memories

↓

Decisions

Now let us take a deeper look into these filters that run our think tank!

Language

Language helps us recognize words depending on whether we understand them in the first place and our previous experience of using them.

Our usage and understanding of words will be decisive in interpreting a message.

For example, the term "How old Cary Grant?" was a journalist's query about Cary Grant's age but the latter understood the message as a query about his health.

Meta programs

Most of us tend to assume everyone is just like we are and we communicate with others the way we want information to be delivered to us. The problem is that everyone doesn't think the way we do and look at things the way we perceive them.

Meta programs are a set of thought and behavior patterns that operate beyond the conscious level. These patterns control one's attention during conversation, habitual linguistic patterns and body language, and so on.

Knowing a person's Meta programs will help you to predict their behavior and actions a lot better.

Since this aspect will help one to communicate specifically in the way an individual needs to receive information. I have dedicated a chapter entirely for this aspect.

Values

Values have a great impact on our motivation.

They shape the way we address people, how we work, listen and evaluate information. They differentiate what is important and what is good or bad for us.

Beliefs

Beliefs correspond to reality and are mostly derived from valid evidence and arguments. Beliefs are the presupposition that we have about the world and things around us.

During a communication it is important to know ones' beliefs as many of the views that come up during a conversation is based on certain sets of beliefs and preconceived notions.

After all, you do not want to talk about Hitler's ideas and his book when conversing about literature with a Jewish friend.

Memories

This filter is all about our recollection of past events.

Memory plays a very important role in human communication. It helps to maintain the thread of a conversation; it ensures that topics are fully discussed.

Moreover, experiences help us react and give feedbacks, whether negative or positive, to certain topics during a conversation.

For example if a budding tennis player was to ask Pete Sampras, "What is so great about Wimbledon?", Sampras would be pleased and would be very happy to share his experiences.

If the youngster asks him about The French Open, Sampras will probably say "It is tough to play in French Open; clay surface is not as comfortable as grass surface."

Here Sampras, a record seven time winner at Wimbledon and French Open struggler, would always have rather bad memories of the French Open, while Wimbledon will always be cherished by him.

Decisions

This is the final filter and is linked closely to memories.

If we have made some good, bad or indifferent decisions in the past we may have created some empowering or disempowering beliefs either about the decision itself or the outcome.

For example, if a woman has had a particularly bad relationship with a man she may say that "All men are the same" and never want to get into a relationship for a long time.

A decision taken by us is expressed in our action and body language.

How Miscommunication Occurs

Once information has been analyzed through our filters, there will be a distortion of information due to deletion as we only pay attention to certain aspects of the information that can be linked to our experiences.

This leads to misrepresentations of the information and an unexpected feedback thus resulting in a miscommunication

Most of us generalize information when we draw conclusions that may be sufficiently different for other people to misunderstand.

If we look at the earlier mentioned example of the woman, we see she has generalized all men as bad at maintaining a good relationship. This is obviously not the case with all men, for if it was, then the world would be one hostile place to live in.

I think it is time we wrap up this chapter.

Before we go into the next chapter, Let us do a recap of what we have learned and refresh our memory with a few exercises.

- **We receive information via one of our senses.**

- **Our filters then determine our internal representation of that event.**

- **It is our internal representation that puts us in a certain state and this in turns creates our physiology.**

- **The state in which we find ourselves, will determine our behavior or reaction to what happens around us.**

Exercises

Appreciating Your Own Values and Those Of Others

Write down all the values and beliefs you have.

For example, what things that you want to experience and have? Success? Freedom? Adventure? Security?

Then, write a list of the things you want to avoid? Rejection? Pain? Failure? Boredom?

Now, have a look at your list and do the same thing for the people who you communicate to the most.

Are you the same? Where do you differ? Build up a mental picture of how they see the world.

This is where we end our first session, hope you got some direction and will continue benefiting from our proceeding sessions.

How to Understand Someone's View of the World

Hello and welcome to the second part of the Effective Communication module.

In this module and the next we are going to look into how people think the way they do and how you should tailor your communication style to meet their view of the world.

Meta Programs

 Just so you can refresh your memory from the previous chapter – Meta Programs are an internal filter that we pass information through.

They are specifically related to the way that we sort and categorize information.

Meta programs go a long way in predicting someone's actions. However, please note that there are no right or wrong Meta programs.

There are several Meta programs but let's go through the top 6 that are used in everyday and business contexts:

- ♦ **Towards/Away from**
- ♦ **Frame of Reference**
- ♦ **Sameness/Difference**
- ♦ **Reason**
- ♦ **Chunk Size**
- ♦ **Convincer**

Towards/away

'Towards people' always strive to achieve an outcome. They want to move towards something.

In their move towards a certain outcome or goal they find it difficult to recognize what should be avoided. Instead they concentrate and focus on what they will get when the outcome is achieved.

On the other hand, 'Away from' people are in an effort to avoid a certain situation. They don't want to experience loss or discomfort and want to move away from something.

Now then, what do you do if you want to know what type of person is someone?

Simple!

Ask them this type of a question:

What do you want? What will having 'xyz' give you? What do you want in 'xyz'?

This is what their response will tell you:

'Toward' people will tell you what they want.

'Away from' people will tell you what they don't want.

Now comes the questions as in how to communicate with people who have a 'Towards' or an 'Away from' strategy.

This is what you do when in *negotiations* with such people:

'Towards'

Work out what their goals are and what you can do to help them achieve these goals. Focus on the outcome and what it will give them.

'Away from'

Work out what you can do to help them avoid what they don't want. Work out and anticipate potential problems and assure them that these can be minimized or avoided.

You can *manage* such people in this fashion:

'Towards'

Offer incentives, i.e. an outcome. Emphasize their goals and what and how they can achieve them.

'Away from'

Use sanctions. Be aware that these people are usually the ones to bring up problems.

<u>Influencing Language</u>

'Towards'

Get, achieve, attain, include, obtain, have, want etc.

'Away from'

Not have, avoid, don't want, keep away from, get rid of etc.

FRAME OF REFERENCE

The second major Meta program is your frame of reference.

This is all about how people evaluate things and can be split out into two:

- ◆ Internal People
- ◆ External People

Internal People stand true to their opinion and evaluate on the basis of what they think is appropriate. They make all decisions themselves and can have difficulty in accepting other people's feedback and direction.

External People, on the other hand, evaluate on the basis of what other people think is appropriate. They need others to guide, direct and motivate them. Since they cannot decide for themselves, they need external references.

So, how do you know if someone is an Internal or an External person?

Ask them this type of question:

How do you know that you have done a good job? How do you know that?

And their response will speak for itself.

Internal people will tell you that they decide when they've done a good job.

External people tell you that they know because other people or outside information sources tell them.

Now when you are in *negotiations* with these people, this is what you should do:

Internal

Emphasize to the person that they will know inside that they are right. Say that they have to decide. Don't bother about external factors or what other people think, they will not be interested in this.

External

Emphasize what others think. Give them data and information to back things up. Give them feedback and reassurance.

Manage these people like this:

Internal

These people have difficulty in accepted feedback or praise. They like to decide for themselves and don't like to be told what to do. They do best when they have little or no supervision. So, just let them be. Don't try to force your opinion down their throat.

External

These people need close management. They need constant feedback and re-assurance about how well they are doing. They need to be told what to do, how to do it and how well they are doing it. Be supportive and encouraging to them.

Influencing language

Internal

You know best, you'll know when it's right, only you can decide, it's up to you etc.

External

Can I give you some feedback, I will let you know, the facts show, other people think that etc.

SAMENESS/DIFFERENCE

This Meta program is all about people's perceptions of likeness and differences.

There are 4 main categories with this:

'Sameness' people will notice those things that are the same or match their previous experiences. They dislike change.

'Sameness with exception' people will first notice the similarities and will then notice the differences. They prefer slow or gradual change.

'Difference with exception' people will notice the differences and then the similarities. They like change and variety.

'Difference' people will notice those things that are different. They love change and want it all of the time.

So, how do you know what type of person they are?

Time to ask them this type of question:

What is the relationship between these three objects? What is the relationship between this X and a previous Y?

What their response will tell you:

'Sameness' people will tell you what similar qualities the objects have.

'Sameness with exception' people will tell you first how things are similar and then tell you what differences they have.

'Difference with exception' people will tell you first how things are different and then give you the similarities.

'Difference' people will plainly tell you what the differences are.

You can use this in the real world in the following manner:

In *negotiations* with these people:

'Sameness'

Stress areas of agreement. Do not discuss differences. Discuss areas of similarities, how you both want the same thing.

'Sameness with exception'

First stress similarities and then point out the differences. Talk about change as a gradual slow process.

'Difference with exception'

First stress how things are different and only then talk about similarities. Focus on change and new solutions

'Difference'

Stress how things are totally different. Do not mention similarities. Talk in terms of massive change and revolutionary.

In *managing* these people:

'Sameness'

Have them do things the same way. They hate variety so don't talk about it. Instead, talk about continuity.
'Sameness with exception'

Have them do the same things but with gradual improvements and changes. Initiate a gradual process of change by talking about it.

'Difference with exception'

Downplay commonality by emphasizing improvements and changes. Stress different ways to do the job and make changes frequently.

'Difference'

Talk about the differences. These people will get bored at repetitive tasks. So have them do something new all the time

Influencing language

'Sameness'

Same, same as, maintain, keep doing, in common, keep the same, usual, similar etc.

'Sameness with exception'

Better, more, less, gradual, although, but, same except etc.

'Difference with exception'

Different, new, changed, change, unusual etc.

'Difference'

Different, new, radical, unique, revolutionary etc.

REASON

The Meta program called Reason is all about people's opinions towards making choices, developing options and following procedures.

Here, there are two types of people:

- ‘Options’
- ‘Procedures’

‘Options’ People are very good at developing choices. They want to experiment and therefore are more of rule breakers or benders than rule followers. They are very good at making improvements and developing new procedures or alternatives to old ones.

‘Procedures’ people are good at following procedures, and thus, are rule followers. But they do not know how to generate them. When they have not got a procedure to follow, they get stuck.

So, here's the question – How do you know what type of a particular person is?

Answer – Ask them this type of question:

Why did you choose xyz?

Their response will tell you:

‘Options’ people will give you the reasons why they did it.

‘Procedures’ people will tell you a story about how they came to do what they did. They don't talk about choices or options. They give you the impression that they don't have choices.

You can use this in the real world:

In n*egotiations* with these people:

‘Options’ People

Do not follow a fixed procedure for the negotiation. Concentrate on the choices and possibilities and discuss all them

‘Procedures’ People

Lay out a procedure for the negotiation. Don't give them with options or choices and don't expect them to decide on alternatives.

In *managing* these people:

'Options' People

Talk about the possibilities and alternatives. Tell them to think of new ways. Do not expect them to follow routines. Make sure that they do not violate procedures.

'Procedures' People

Stress the procedures to do the work. Make sure there are procedures in place and that the person understands them. Be prepared to assist if the procedure fails.

Influencing Language

'Options' People

Alternatives, reasons, options, choices, possibilities etc.

'Procedures' People

Correct way, procedure, known way, right way, proven way etc.

CHUNK SIZE

The need for details in an individual's life throws two categories of people at us—one, the detailed or specific person, and two, those who prefer large chunks of information or the global person.

Specific people like to work with all the small details. They like to understand and go into pieces of work with the minutest of detail.

In contrast, Global people like to talk in big pictures and are not interested in details at all. They are conceptual and abstract. They'd rather give you the overall framework or brief of what is happening than go into details.

You know when someone is specific and when someone is global just by asking them any question and analyzing their response.

Specific people will give you all the details and go to great lengths to explain everything when you ask questions. Specific people become frustrated with Global People because there is no detail in what they say.

However, Global people give you an overview without details. They tend to use large generalizations. Global people become frustrated with Specific people because they go too far into detail.

Apply this to the real world:

In *negotiations* with these people:

Specific

Avoid generalizations and vagueness. Break things down into the detail and be specific. Present things in logical sequences.

Global

Avoid details and present the bigger picture.

In *managing* these people:

Specific

Tell the person in detail what needs to be done and ensure that there is a logical sequence. Do not expect them to think about the bigger picture

Global

Skip the details and give the person a broad overview. Tell them what the end game is and let them fill in the rest.

<u>Influencing Language</u>

Specific

Next, then, precisely, exactly, specifically, first, second, details etc.

Global

Big picture, framework, in brief, result, generally, overview etc.

CONVINCER

People make decisions and are convinced for only one of four reasons:

It looks right
 It feels right
  It sounds right
   It makes sense

How do you find out what kind of person uses what reason to make a decision?

Ask them this question:

Why did you decide xyz?

What their response will tell you:

The 'Looks right' people do things because the representation that they make to themselves is a picture that literally looks right. They will use visual words when describing their decision.

The 'Feel right' people do things because the representation they make to themselves is a sensation in some part of their body which literally feels right. They use kinesthetic words when describing their decision.

'Sounds right' people do things because the representation they make to themselves is a series of words which literally sounds right to them. They will use auditory words when describing their decision.

'Makes sense' people do things because the representation they make to themselves is based on logic which in their own mind, they know, is correct. They will use auditory words when describing their decision and they will use facts, data and reason.

Utilize it in the real world:

In *negotiations* with these people:

Use the appropriate language patterns that match their decision process. If you are providing learning materials, make sure they are appropriate for the person – i.e. pictures, diagrams, facts, data etc.

In *managing* these people:

'Looks right'

Paint a picture in words, draw a diagram, and give them pictorial references to explain things to them. Let their imagination flow free. Show them how to do it.

'Feels right'

Get their internal senses working by letting them discern what they have to do. Let them get their hands on the task under supervision, and touch, feel and experience what needs to be done.

'Sounds right'

Have them describe to themselves in internal dialogue or in an appropriate tone of voice what they are supposed to do. Tell them things. Tell them what others say. They will make decisions after exploring all that they have heard.

'Makes sense'

They are the logical ones, so give them reasons for what you want them to do. Let them read instructions on how to do the job. Give them facts, statistics and data.

Influencing language

Use appropriate language, as in, what suits each type of person to help them make their decisions. (We are going to look into this in greater detail in the next chapter)

Time for some action. Here's an exercise to test what you have learnt till now.

* EXERCISE *

ELICITING META-PROGRAMMES

Part 1:

Now that you have seen what makes up each of the Meta programs, what preferences do you have?

Take time out to read through each again and write down below what your own Meta programs are for your self-awareness and why?

- ◆ Towards/Away

- ◆ Frame of Reference

- ◆ Sameness/Difference

- ◆ Reason

- ◆ Chunk Size

- ◆ Convincer

Part 2:

The next step is that in the coming week, listen very hard to your colleagues and friends and elicit their Meta programs.

Write these down and then formulate a strategy of how best to communicate to a few selected persons.

How to Communicate With Different Types of People

Greetings! Friend...

You have reached the third part of the Effective Communication course.

In the previous chapter you learnt how to enter other people's "world" while communicating with them, so that you are at par with them and are able to work with them comfortably.

Your communication skills, in fact, have jumped a few scales above now and armed with this new talent you can nearly rule the roost!

Internal Representational Systems

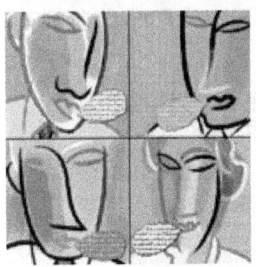 From the earlier chapters, you must already be familiar with making internal representations and Convincer, a Meta program that describes the way people think and what they base their decisions on. We have also described that information comes in one of 5 main senses.

Well, it is now time to put all of this together by recognizing the thinking process of a person. This, we will accomplish by listening to the verbal indicators that they use in everyday speech and then using this information to design the way we communicate with them.

Remember, people like people who are like themselves!

For example, if Greg and Lily meet for the first time at a party, they will hit it off easily if both are the "It looks right" decision-making people. Since they both use mainly visual indicators they will find it easier to communicate and explain things to each other by showing real objects or by painting a diagram or by creating a picture in their minds' eye.

So, below is a list of indicators of the words that people use for the 3 main modalities:

Visual	Auditory	Kinesthetic	Unspecified
See	Hear	Fell	Sense
Look	Listen	Touch	Experience
View	Sounds	Grasp	Understand
Appear	Make music	Get hold of	Think
Show	Harmonize	Slip through	Learn
Dawn	Tune in/out	Catch on	Process
Reveal	Be all ears	Tap into	Decide

You Said What?

Envision	Rings a bell	Make contact	Motivate
Illuminate	Silence	Throw out	Consider
Imagine	Be heard	Turn around	Change
Clear	Resonate	Hard	Perceive
Foggy	Deaf	Unfeeling	Insensitive
Focused	Mellifluous	Concrete	Distinct
Hazy	Dissonance	Get a handle	Know
Picture	Unhearing	Solid	

Below is a list of indicator phrases that people use. Which ones do you use most often?

Visual	Auditory	Kinesthetic
An eyeful	Afterthought	All washed up
Appears to me	Blabbermouth	Boils down to
Beyond a shadow of a doubt	Call on	Chip off the old block
Birds eye view	Clear as a bell	Come to grips with
Catch a glimpse of	Clearly expressed	Control yourself
Clear cut	Describe in detail	Cool/calm/collected
Dim view	Earful	Firm foundations
Flashed on	Enquire into	Get a handle on
Get a perspective on	Give me your ear	Get a load of this
Get a scope on	Give you a call	Get in touch with
Hazy idea	Given amount of	Get the drift of
In light of	Grant an audience	Get your back up
In person	Heard voices	Hand in hand
In view of	Hidden message	Hand in there
Looks like	Hold your tongue	Heated argument
Make a scene	Ideal talk	Hold it
Mental image	Key note speaker	Hold on
Mental picture	Loud and clear	Hot head
Minds eye	Manner of speaking	Keep your shirt on
Naked eye	Pay attention to	Lay cards on the table
Paint a picture	Power of speech	Pain in the neck
See to it	State your purpose	Pull some strings
Short sighted	To tell the truth	Sharp as a tack
Showing off	Tongue-tied	Slipped my mind
Sight for sore eyes	Tuned in/tuned out	Smooth operator
Staring off into space	Unheard of	So-so
Take a peak	Utterly	Start from scratch
Tunnel vision	Voiced an opinion	Stuff upper lip
Under your nose	Well informed	Stuffed shirt
Up front	Within hearing	Too much hassle
Well defined	Word for word	Topsy-turvy

* EXERCISE *

YOUR REPRESENTATIONAL SYSTEM

What words do you use the most?

How do you think?

How would you best learn a new material? Through a diagram? By listening? Or by doing and feeling?

What category do you fit into the most?

Think about your friends and colleagues at work. What modalities do they use?

If you know that someone is visual – when communicating with him/her you should draw a picture or diagram and use phrases such as "Can you see it?" and "Just imagine" etc.

Eliciting thinking patterns through eye movement

Researchers, in the late seventies and early eighties, discovered that people move their eyes in a certain way when they think.

It was also noticed that students, when asked a series of questions, had structured pattern eye movements while thinking.

Researchers therefore concluded that by looking at someone's eyes, you could tell how they think.

It is true that you can tell the way people are constructing their thoughts by observing their eye movements.

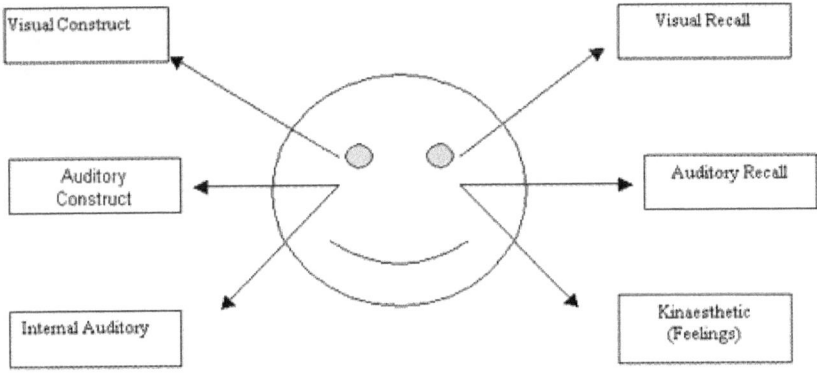

The above picture is how a person looks when you are facing him/her.

The basic rule of eye movement pattern works this way:

Direction	Meaning
Looking up	Visualizing
Looking horizontally to left and right	Remembering or constructing sounds
Looking down to left	Accessing feelings
Looking down to right	Talking to self

Visual Recall

This is when you are recalling images from the past. You are drawing them from your memory and these are things you have seen before.

Questions to ask?

"What did your curtains look like when you were a teenager?"
"What does your car look like?"
"What was your nanny's name?"

Visual Construct

This happens when you are visualizing something you have never seen before. These are images you are making up in your head.

Sometimes you can use this one to see if people are lying to you!

Questions to ask?

"What would your car look like if it had a soft top?"
"What would your house look like if it were painted red?"
"What would you look like if you lost 3 stone in weight?"

Auditory Recall

This is when you remember sounds or voices that you have heard before or things that you have said to yourself before. These sounds are stored in your memory bank and you are actually extracting it from its location.

It's this ability that helps you recognize a voice over the phone even before the person says his/her name.

Questions to ask?

"Can you remember the sound of your grandfather's voice?"
"Can you remember what you said to yourself when you stole that pie from the oven?"
"What was the last thing I said?"

Auditory Construct

This is when you are making up sounds that you have never heard before.

Questions to ask?

"What would the national anthem sound like if it were played on the flute?"
"What would I sound like if I were fluent in Spanish?"

Kinesthetic

This involves accessing your feelings.

Questions to ask?

"What does it feel like to touch this sand paper?"
"What does it feel like to be so popular?"

Internal Auditory

This is where your eyes go when you are having internal dialogue and talking to yourself.

Questions to ask?

"Will you be able to get through this interview without getting nervous?"
"Can you recite 'Three Lions' to yourself?"

Since communication is all about rapport building, we have to be able to mirror and match another person's preferred learning and thinking style.

By observing words that people use and how they move their eyes we can understand their strategy. However, don't always look for strategies in people's eyes. This is because not all eye movements indicate one.

However, in order to communicate effectively we need to study action signals put forward by people and then modify our behavior, physiology and words so that they can easily relate to us.

After all, that is what effective communication is all about, right?

Okay, that's it for this module!

See you next time with how to build up rapport with anyone and how to put together everything you have learned so far.

You Said What?

Good luck!

How To Be A Great Communicator And Build Up Rapport Effortlessly

Building Rapport

You meet different types of people everyday. It is not possible to make and maintain a good relationship with all of them. No one clicks with every person he/she meets. However, it's important for you to create positive interactions with those who can push your buttons.

Communication needs to be result oriented. Building rapport is the ultimate tool for producing results and is vital for effective communication. The foundation for any meaningful interaction, it makes you more memorable and can be critical in your personal life and career.

Building rapport is similar to building a bridge over a river. The stronger the bridge, the more it can carry. In a relationship, you can ask for more if you have better rapport with the other person.

Irrespective of your knowledge about the person, there are 6 main steps to establish rapport with anyone.

Communication is much more than exchange of words. In fact, 93% of all communication is down to the tonality of your voice and your body language. So, building rapport is far more than just talking about common experiences.

However, people like people when they resemble themselves. When they don't, it

is difficult to have any kind of relationship, let alone an effective one!

Some people easily build rapport with others. Take a look into your past. Was building rapport an easy a job for you?

Even if you are a master rapport builder, for sure you've also had times when you thought, "Oh, what am I going to do and say next?"

Everyone has such experiences.

Or consider an entirely different situation. You are so tired and have a terrible headache. Then a friend or colleague comes jumping in and full of energy, wanting to talk your head off?

There have also been times, for sure, when you turned out to be the irritating friend.

Ok, let's take a look at the 6 things you need to do to build rapport.

1. Match the persons sensory modality

People like to have relationship with those who think and behave like themselves, or even with those who have similar background. Matching and mirroring the way others think and talk is a good way to build rapport with them.

There is slight difference between mirroring and matching. Mirroring is quite similar to looking into a mirror. The time difference between the actions of both parties is negligible. However, in matching you would have to wait for your turn to repeat the action of the other party.

Take a look at the portion about visual, auditory and kinesthetic modalities. It's time for you to put it into practice.

Take note of the indicator words that the person is using and use words/phrases from the same modality. Also, look out for eye movements to spot thinking patterns.

2. Mirror the persons Physiology

Have you ever noticed that a group of teenagers who are friends bear similarities in their clothing, vocabulary and movements? People who are in rapport have a tendency to dress in a similar way or have matching body language.

Mirroring the physiology of someone you're talking to can make him/her feel comfortable. Copying the person's posture, facial expressions, hand gestures, movements and even their eye blinking, will cause their body to say unconsciously to their mind that this person is like me!

3. Matching their voice

You should match the tone, tempo, timbre and the volume of the person's voice. If the person is slow and deliberate, he will feel comfortable if you are the same way. You should also try, when you speak, to use the keywords that they use a lot.

For examples: "Alright", "Actually", "You know what I mean"

4. Matching their breathing

If there is a big difference in the breathing pattern of two people in conversation, both of them would feel uncomfortable. If you want to build rapport with someone, you need to match the rhythm of breathing of the other person by moving your foot or finger at the same pace.

5. Matching how they deal with information

Different people deal with information differently. Some are detail oriented and some prefer it brief. You need to match the other person's way of dealing with information.

If you get this wrong you will find it very difficult to build rapport as the detailed oriented person will be yearning for more information and the other type of person will soon be yawning!

6. Matching common experiences

Suppose, you are a long way from home and met someone, who is a total stranger, and discovered he is from your own hometown. Before long, you will find yourself in a very lively conversation with the guy, looking for experiences in common.

Consider the opposite case. You are in a restaurant and everybody at your table has been served their food but you. How do you feel? Out of place?

This is all about finding some commonality. If both parties have matching experiences, interests, backgrounds, values and beliefs, they have greater chance to be in rapport.

One point to bear in mind is that you need to be subtle when you are matching and mirroring. Be careful not to exceed the limits. Typically, however, the other person will not notice it.

You can develop your ability to observe other people to such an extent that you will begin to see and even predict people's reactions to communications. This is known as calibration and is a way of determining whether you are in rapport with someone.

<u>Increasing levels of rapport</u>

Matching Modalities

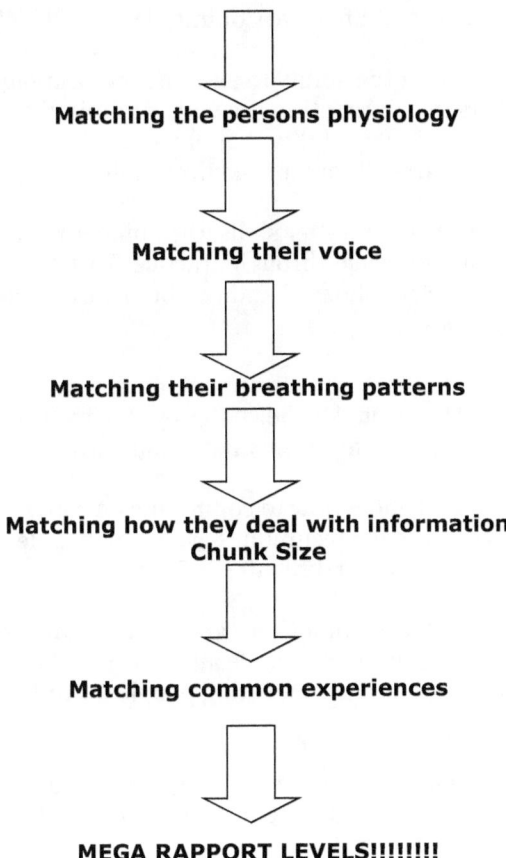

Matching the persons physiology

Matching their voice

Matching their breathing patterns

Matching how they deal with information Chunk Size

Matching common experiences

MEGA RAPPORT LEVELS!!!!!!!!

That's it for this module!

Don't forget to try it all out!!

How to Make Small Talk with People

Welcome to part 5 of Effective Communication Skills!

"The gift of gab" or the ability to enter a new or unfamiliar situation and begin to engage others in conversation is a widely admired skill. Many people wrongly consider it as an innate ability that one is born with. The ability to make small talk is not a natural gift but an acquired skill.

One of the most sought-after skills, the ability to make successful small talk can be learned and perfected through practice. This skill can play a vital role in boosting your self confidence and can be critical in your personal and professional life.

For most people, starting a conversation with unfamiliar people is a difficult and painful task. They would rather pull their toe nails out than actually have to go up to someone they have never met before and strike up a conversation!

This session is all about how to communicate with people you have never met before. You can use the techniques even with people whom you find really incommunicative or in a difficult situation.

Meeting people for the first time can be a very daunting task. However, if you understand all about other people and how they like to communicate and what they like to talk about, then meeting people for the first time can be an enjoyable experience.

The main difficulty you face in starting a small talk with an unfamiliar person is that you put yourself under tremendous pressure to talk. You will start asking yourself questions like:

What should **I** talk about?

What shall **I** say?

How will **I** fill this silence in the conversation?

You are very concerned about how others are evaluating you while you are making small talk. You are concerned not only for the evaluation during the talk but also for the judgment that goes beyond the conversation. You are too busy thinking of what to say that you forget about communicating with the other person!

BECOME AN EXPERT LISTENER

"You say it best when you say nothing at all"
                    Boyzone

The best conversationalists in this world are the best listeners. You must resist the urge to dominate the conversation. In fact, the person who says the least is often the best communicator. Then why should you be racking your brains thinking of things to say every time?

In a conversation, you are listening means the other person is talking. Becoming an expert listener makes you a good conversationalist. During the conversation lean slightly forward, face the other person directly, and don't miss a single word. Most people are poor listeners because they are busy preparing a reply while the other person is still speaking.

When you go into a situation where you are meeting someone for the first time, you need to be very much focused on him/her. You must treat that person as if he/she is the most important person in the world. Ask questions that evoke interest in them and be intrigued about them.

Small talks depend very much on your ability to ask questions and to listen attentively to the answers. Wait for your turn to speak. The others person will ask about you at any point during the conversation. Don't talk for too long. Always try to ask open-ended questions.
So, how can you start and hold a good conversation?

To do this, it is important to understand what other people like to talk about. Here is the TOP 5 in order:

1. THEMSELVES!

You know how much you love to talk about how you dribbled the ball and beat three defenders in a row yesterday or about your high grades in the last exam.

Yes, people love to talk about themselves.

The best way to build rapport with someone and to hold a conversation is letting them to talk about their favorite subject - THEMSELVES!

Always ask for their opinion, their stand and more importantly about their achievements.

Suppose you are the representative of a magazine and you want to get the opinion of a business person. How will you start the conversation if you ran into him one day?

Normally you will start like, "Hello, my name is…" Once you reveal your identity the person will try to keep away from you.

What if you start the conversation like, "Hello Mr. Jobs. So you made it to the BOD of Avalon Inc?" Mr. Jobs will surely have something to say about it.

Ask question to get them to talk about themselves and then ask some more questions, and then some more!

He or she will love you for it!

2. THEIR OWN OPINIONS

An opinion is something everyone has got. And people love to air their one on anything and everything.

"What do you think of the way Manchester United has played this year?"
"What is your opinion on the strike?"
"What do you think of XYZ program?"

Ask these questions, you will have your new friend talking for hours!

Be careful not to be argumentative even if your opinion differs. However, if you want to conclude, you can make a sharp exit by refuting his opinion.

3. OTHER PEOPLE

Who doesn't want to gossip?

People love to talk about other people. You can easily start a conversation by talking about someone the other party has an interest in.

"Heard your niece is the new Ms California. Is she planning for a career in modeling?"

You will get everything from how much the niece loves the person to her appointments till 2050.

4. THINGS

"I love YOUR car, what model is it?"

All are proud of their possessions and never spoil a chance to talk about them. You will surely get a detailed description of the vehicle for the above question.

You can also start an interesting conversation by mentioning about anything that can evoke an interest in the other party. You know how long two teenage boys can talk about girls.

5. YOU!

So you have reached the bottom of the list. It's quite unfortunate that the last thing people want to talk about is YOU!

As you are trying to keep the conversation focused on the other person, you will have to wait for your turn to speak about yourself. And worse, you cannot talk about what you want to. Whatever you say should be connected to what the other person has already said.

Following is an action plan to start and hold a conversation. Try it out next time.

ACTION PLAN

- **You don't have to think munch or worry about what to say. Just have an idea of the other person and go ahead.**
- **Carefully listen and ask relevant questions about the other person.**
- **Then you can take some liberty and ask some more questions!**
- **Always think about "YOU" instead of "I."**
- **Find the other person's favorite 5 subjects and talk about them in order!**
- **Don't talk about yourself until the other person asks.**
- **Have a lot of fun!**

Making the first move

You are in a party and whenever that tall girl with brown hair smiles your heart skips a beat. You want to make the first move, but you don't have the courage.

Your brain is in search of the hundred reasons why the girl will not like you. You are sure that you will be rejected because there are better men. And worse, you have nothing to say to the girl. Simply you are scared.

Not an unfamiliar situation, right?

What if the girl is thinking exactly the same thing?

Never spoil a chance to make the first move. You don't have to worry about or be scared of a possible rejection. Take a deep breath, go to the person and ask an opening question.

When you meet a person at a particular place you can be sure of one thing. Some common interests brought both of you there. And you know how to start and hold a conversation with someone who shares some interests with you.

Small talk is the foundation of any serious conversation. So it's always good to start off with small talk. Start on simple topics of conversation and then move on.

**"There are no uninteresting people,
only disinterested listeners!"**

Okay! That's it for this module!

Don't forget to try out the tips!

Giving and Receiving Feedback

Welcome to the final part of the communications course, I hope you have enjoyed it.

This chapter is all about giving and receiving feedback.

Giving feedback

Feedback is a powerful communication tool. It can help people know their behavior and find out things about themselves that they might not have considered. The ability to give and solicit feedback makes you a good communicator.

Giving feedback is one of the most difficult things in communication. Some people struggle with giving proper feedback in their personal and professional lives. Without knowing how to give feedback, it can be uncomfortable and unpleasant for both the giver and the receiver.

A feedback should be given in a way that the receiver can use it to either make improvements or keep up the good work. This communication tool is widely used in education and is essential for learning and continuous improvement. Constructive feedbacks motivate people.

A corrective feedback is supposed to relay specific information that provides the recipient guidance and direction in an activity. Many people find it difficult to give corrective feedback. However, it is possible to learn techniques for effectively offering both praise and correction.

Giving feedback is an integral part of the coaching process that provides your staff members with support and direction, and ultimately results in increased participation. Both positive and negative feedbacks have their part to play. It is the best way to convey your staff what you think about a particular work or performance.

Principles of feedback

Following are the seven principles of feedback.

1. Choose correct timing for feedback

Feedback is most helpful and effective when given at the earliest opportunity after the given behavior or incident has occurred. Immediate feedback will help to reinforce a correct behavior and make it more likely to happen again.

Corrective feedback also is the most effective when given as soon as possible. If a wrong behavior is not corrected with corrective feedback at the earliest possible moment, the staff member may repeat it and set a bad precedence. However, in the case of corrective feedback, the receiver's willingness to hear it is very important.

2. Ask for self assessment

In a communication process, the willingness of the receiver to hear the feedback is very important. To ensure the participation of the other party, the sender needs to create an open atmosphere before giving a corrective feedback.

Asking the person for self-assessment may help involve him/her in the feedback process. It can create an open atmosphere and promote dialogue between the sender and the receiver. In fact, few people are not aware of the gravity of the mistakes they have committed or the job they have done well.

Allowing the person to voice his/her opinions before providing your own assessment of performance can lead to more positive results. Such opportunities for self assessment may help the person to gradually assume more responsibility without supervision.

3. Focus on specifics

"I liked the way you trained your subordinate. You outlined the procedure in writing and then listened as he relayed back to you the process. Great job!"

Take a look at the above statement.

Feedbacks should not be linked to the personality or character of the person. You should focus on a specific correct or incorrect behavior. Such feedbacks can make the person more willing and able to change. A feedback should be specific, visible and measurable in order to be effective.

For example, when providing corrective feedback:

Do: "When you were talking to customer xyz, I noticed that you forgot to use her name"

Don't: "You are not building rapport with the customer"

When providing praise:

Do: "When you spoke to customer xyz, I noticed that you used really good open and closed questioning techniques"

Don't: "You communicated well there"

4. Limit feedback to a few important points

A feedback should address the needs of you and the other person. However, it should be limited to a few very important points.

Good coaches and communicators identify one or two critical areas and help the person address them one at a time. Examination of many aspects of behavior at one time is too hard to be effective.

Restrict your feedback to one or two important points so that you do not overwhelm the other person with too many things to consider.

5. Provide more praise than corrective feedback

Praise is usually given for exemplary work or behavior that exceeds expectations. However, positive reinforcement can always play an important role in bringing about change. The sad thing is that people always focus on negatives.

When you give corrective feedback, remember to point out correct behaviors first. This is as important as pointing out mistakes and areas that need improvement. And always try to conclude the conversation in a positive manner.

6. Give praise for expected performance

Some times a positive appraisal or a word of praise can make miracles. Praise is a strong motivator and nothing is more encouraging than acceptance.

People deserve to be praised for doing their job to the expected level. In fact, positive feedbacks are enjoyable for both the sender and the receiver.

One thing you have to keep in mind is that praising anyone who meets established standards is as important as praising the exceptional performer. Tell the person exactly why you are praising him/her in clear and specific words.

Remember, praise may be what it takes to turn an average employee into an exceptional one.

7. Develop Action Plans

Effective implementation of any process needs an action plan. You need to work together with subordinates to identify the desired performance or result and how it can be achieved. Also decide a deadline for the completion of the steps.

Useful techniques to use when giving feedback

Following are some useful techniques you can use in feedback sessions:

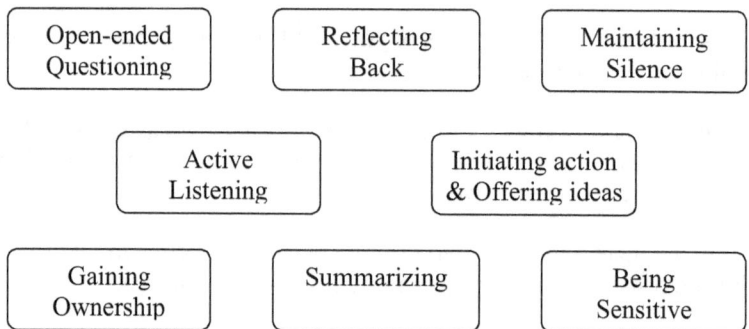

Open-ended questioning

Open-ended questions do not have a preset limit. They promote continued conversation and allow the person to give more details. They are meant to draw out more information and often give more insight into the other person's feelings.

Consider the following question.

"Do you like the new program?"

The question can be answered with a yes or no, or with a simple statement of fact.

What about asking the following question instead?

"What are your concerns about this new program?"

Use words like:
What?
How?
Who?
Tell me?

Avoid closed questions when you are trying to get more information from someone.

Avoid words like:
Do you?
Did you?
Have you?

Also be careful with the use of the word "Why," especially when you are giving feedback. The person may think that you are blaming him/her or being critical if you use it.

Reflecting Back

You can use the other person's complaints as a tool to create an open atmosphere. This is about putting what the other person has said into your own words and reflecting it back. This technique is known as paraphrasing.

Paraphrasing is a good way to show that you are listening and more importantly that you are listening and understanding!

For example:

The other person – "I always seem to get the rough end of the stick - no-one listens to me at all…….."

You – "You seem concerned that no-one listens to you and that you seem to be getting a dumb deal"

Maintaining Silence

You can convey a lot of things via silence. Moreover, you can encourage the person to take his/her time and give an appropriate reply. Always give the other person time to think through their reply.

Silence is not an opportunity to feel uncomfortable or lose your interest in the conversation. Be careful to maintain eye contact and demonstrate an interest.

Summarizing

The other person needs to be convinced that you have heard everything correctly and understood from his/her perspective. Summarize the output of the meeting and action plan and recite it to him/her.

Then you can conclude the discussion and focus on planning for the future.

Example: "The three major issues you raised were……"
        "To summarize then……"

Being Sensitive

A good communicator is an empathetic person. Being sensitive to the needs of the person is important as they may reject the feedback initially. Give the person space and time to think. This may help him/her to absorb the feedback in its true sense.

Initiating Action and Offering Ideas

Feedback is always associated with improvement. So giving a well-structured action plan and some ideas for the betterment of the performance can be very constructive.

Consider the following example.

"Can you think of an action that would help build on your skills in this area?"

Do not allow your personal opinion to reflect in the ideas you offer. You have many other opportunities to do that.

Gaining Ownership

You need to make the person feel comfortable to act in line with your feedback. For this, you can help him/her to integrate the feedback into his/her experience. Then he/she can have a point of view other than yours.

Linking the feedback as much as possible to business results and objectives will help increase ownership. Remember, any change in behavior will only occur through acceptance and ownership of the feedback by that person.

Receiving Feedback

There are times when you face the other side of the coin too. While giving feedback, remember that some time or the other you will also be at, let's just call it the 'receiving end'. So be prepared.

Etch this onto your mind- As long as the feedback comes to you in a non-judgmental and appropriate fashion accept it is as a valuable piece of information for learning and for our continued development as a person.

This valuable piece of 'information' is what we call constructive feedback and it is critical for self-development and growth.

Here are some points to remember when you receive feedback:

Don't shy away from constructive feedback, welcome it

- Accept feedback of any sort for what it is – information
- Evaluate the feedback before responding
- Make your own choice about what you intend to do with the information

The feedback emotional rollercoaster

Here's a feedback model that you should keep in mind while giving or receiving feedback.

D A W A

DENIAL

This is typically associated with jumping the gun. Most people while receiving feedback tend to jump at it and immediately get defensiveness by arguing, denying or justifying. Try to avoid it. This just gets in the way of appreciation of the information you are being given.

ANGER

So you've been told that your work is not as good as what it ought to be. Here comes Anger! Coming right after denial where you said, "It's as good as always", you get angry as the feedback stews in your mind and body. The immediate reaction is to fume!

WITHDRAWAL

Once the anger dies down, people get time to reflect and ponder on the feedback. "Well, I have been making more mistakes then normal" This is when time is taken out to mull over the feedback and think about what it actually means.

ACCEPTANCE

The withdrawal stage is closely followed by the final part of this model – accepting the feedback, assessing its value and the consequences of ignoring it, or using it. "I HAVE been making mistakes."

That's it for this module and the course! Trust you have enjoyed it!

Remember to use the tips.

Also be sure to take advantage of our one-on-one personal coaching programs as well as personal counseling.

More information on our coaching programs can be discovered as you visit our coaching portal at www.CoachingWithWayne.com

Can you imagine your life fully on track and accomplishing all that you have desired? Be sure to check us out today!